THEN & NOW

FORT SHERIDAN

Opposite: Building No. 9 was built for the fort's commander and his family. While there are no names to accompany this photograph, these would have been the elite of Fort Sheridan gathered at this home.

THEN & NOW

FORT SHERIDAN

Laura Tucker

To my husband, Master Chief John B. (Brian) Tucker, for devoting your life to the United States Navy and for bringing me to Fort Sheridan, where our life together began. And to our twins, Jack and Payton. You are the loves of my life and my inspiration. I know Fort Sheridan will always hold a special place in your hearts.

Copyright © 2008 by Laura Tucker
ISBN 978-0-7385-5191-3

Library of Congress control number: 2007940130

Published by Arcadia Publishing
Charleston SC, Chicago IL, Portsmouth NH, San Francisco CA

Printed in the United States of America

For all general information contact Arcadia Publishing at:
Telephone 843-853-2070
Fax 843-853-0044
E-mail sales@arcadiapublishing.com
For customer service and orders:
Toll-Free 1-888-313-2665

Visit us on the Internet at www.arcadiapublishing.com

On the front cover: Then and now activities of Fort Sheridan are as different as these two photographs. A calm, cool autumn day on the parade grounds is a typical modern-day scene for this private community. But by comparison, it is a stark contrast to the U.S. Army's marching soldiers and horses parading their patriotism for a pass and review ceremony in the early days. That is, after all, for which this beautiful place was created. (Contemporary image, author's collection; vintage image, courtesy of the Lake County Discovery Museum.)

On the back cover: The horse arena at Fort Sheridan provided a stage for the U.S. cavalry to display its extraordinary riding skills. At events like this one, around 1920, local socialites would gather to take in the spectacle held on the parade grounds. Once the main attraction, the thunderous roar of the horses and applause has long since faded. (Courtesy of the Lake County Discovery Museum.)

CONTENTS

Acknowledgments

Brian, thanks for being supportive throughout this endeavor and understanding the importance that it holds for me.

Thank you Diana Dretske and the Lake County Discovery Museum for all your help with obtaining past images for my book and providing answers to my many questions.

Michael Mariano, thank you for taking the time to escort me to the top of the water tower to shoot some of the photographs.

Lawrence Noble, the sculptor, thank you for allowing me use your wonderful creation of Gen. Philip Henry Sheridan as the muse for my logo. It is much appreciated.

Special thanks to Cyndi Dawson for watching Jack and Payton all day while I was shooting for the book and to Bob Drinkall for shooting those last-minute photographs for me. Your friendship and the friendship of our children will always be special to us.

Unless otherwise noted, the vintage images are courtesy of the Lake County Discovery Museum in Wauconda and the Library of Congress and the contemporary images are courtesy of the author's collection.

INTRODUCTION

Some call it a landmark, some call it home, but surely all who know it, call it remarkable. Fort Sheridan was home to U.S. Army troops and military families from 1887 until the base closure in 1993 gave it a new lease on life and began its transformation into what is now a prestigious North Shore community, just 25 miles from downtown Chicago.

This book was created with the intention of highlighting the history of the northern historic section of the fort as well as presenting the present by comparing what was with what is. To truly understand and appreciate Fort Sheridan for what it is today, one must look back to where it has been.

Fort Sheridan is named after Gen. Philip Henry Sheridan, a United States cavalry soldier and Civil War hero. It was created out of necessity in 1887 after the Great Chicago Fire of 1871, the railway labor strikes of 1877, and the Haymarket Riot of 1886. All of this strife prompted the wealthy businessmen of Chicago and the North Shore to convince the government to establish a permanent post nearby for security. Members of the Commercial Club of Chicago arranged for the acquisition of 632 acres for this purpose. Part of this parcel was a large farm along Lake Michigan owned by the Kilgare family. It was just outside Highwood. Sheridan was also a member of the Commercial Club and played an integral role in restoring order after the Great Chicago Fire. The fort, formerly known as Camp Highwood, was officially named Fort Sheridan by order of Pres. Grover Cleveland. Sheridan signed the order himself, and on February 27, 1888, it was renamed. The first commanding officer of Fort Sheridan was Maj. William Lyster.

The first 64 buildings were designed by the Chicago architectural firm of Holabird and Roche. The look of Fort Sheridan is unique as the brilliant architecture is paired with the creamy yellow brick made right on-site with clay mined from the bluffs along Lake Michigan. Trimmed with swirling, black wrought iron fixtures, the buildings are as beautiful as they are functional. The landscaping and building placement was designed by landscape architect Ossian C. Simonds. He created the prairie effect on the parade grounds by placing trees in a way that makes the grounds seem even more expansive when looking east and in the fall creates a wondrous display of colors. The natural ravines were an important element in the consideration of building placement. Simonds wanted to preserve the integrity of nature as much as possible.

While the interiors of most of the structures have been completely remodeled to accommodate the modern uses for them, the exterior of the buildings have been preserved. Fort Sheridan was added to the National Register of Historic Places in 1980 and in 1984 became a national historic landmark. It is a perfect example of restoration and preservation, and its stories can be told to generations to come.

Through the past 120 years, thousands have called this beautiful place home, if only for a short time. Servicemen and servicewomen and their families have enjoyed the expansive 230-acre site for both work and play. The last military families were relocated to the new construction in the southern section of the fort after the closing of noncommissioned officers housing on Westover Road in late 2007.

Fort Sheridan will surely leave a lasting impression on all who have entered through its gates. It is rich in history, natural vegetation, and recreation, complete with walking and bicycle trails, a community beach, and even outdoor museum exhibits. It boasts both beautiful architecture and natural wonders living in perfect harmony. It has undergone many changes on the way to this picture-perfect state as one will see while traveling through the fort in this pictorial journey from the past to the present.

THE WATER TOWER AND BARRACKS

The water tower and barracks were among the first structures at Fort Sheridan. Built in 1891 at a height of 227 feet, the tower rivaled the skyscrapers in downtown Chicago in height for that era. It is still one of the tallest buildings on the North Shore. With the inclusion of the barracks, the entire structure is 1,005 feet long. They are officially known as buildings No. 48, No. 49, and No. 50. Facing north toward the parade grounds, they are the very essence of the fort.

From the south, this photograph, gives a clear view of a dirt road leading to the rear of the tower. The opening in the tower's base was created for traffic to pass through. At that time, it mostly consisted of horses and soldiers. Now the road is paved and the bridge reconstructed. The opening remains, but the concrete barriers allow only foot and bicycle traffic to enter into the tower's base. The rear side of the tower is distinguished from the front by the four windows cascading down the right side.

Another southern view of the tower, this c. 1914 photograph, marks the beginning of one transformation of the tower and barracks into part of Lovell General Hospital, named for Joseph Lovell, surgeon general of the army from 1818 to 1836. The tower's opening was blocked, making it almost unrecognizable at ground level. In this photograph from 2006, the temporary structure has left no reminders of its presence, and the base of the tower is once again open to cool breezes and passersby.

With the barracks on the right and the kitchens on the left, this view from the east in 1917 shows an alley between the buildings. The mess hall was actually across the street directly behind the kitchens. These days, the ground level has been eliminated by a large deck that extends the length of the barracks to the tower. Underneath is an entrance to the private parking garage for the residents who now occupy the barracks refurbished as townhomes.

This view of Whistler Road, looking east around 1930, is not only dated by the cars but also by the height of the tower. The single structures on the left are the wings of the barracks in the rear. They no longer have entrances from Whistler Road, as shown here in the current photograph; instead garages were added to provide a modern-day convenience for the residents. (Contemporary image, courtesy of Bob Drinkall.)

In 1930, as shown here, there were quite a few noticeable differences in the appearance of Leonard Wood Avenue South. For one, the parade grounds housed a building that can been seen on the far left in the early photograph. There were more telephone poles than trees, and the roads were unpaved, giving it an overall rustic appearance. Today the same street looks polished, and the new light fixtures and street signs look as though they could have been here all along.

INFANTRY AND CAVALRY BARRACKS, FORT SHERIDAN ILL.

In 1949, the water tower was lowered by 58 feet due to a structural weakness in the roof. It stands today at 169 feet. The outdoor kiosk along the paved walking trail that wraps itself halfway around the parade grounds details the renovation on "the Fort's Icon." It is still used today for its original purpose, as an elevated water storage tank. Inside there is a 90,000-gallon steel tank that supplies water for the fort. The journey from the base to the top is 225 spiraling steps.

Newly constructed, the water tower and barracks stand tall and proud in this photograph. With windows too numerous to count, every detail is crafted with precision. Terra-cotta-colored roof tiles adorn the creamy yellow building with the steeplelike chimney pipes peeking out of the top. The architect's design is realized. A less ornate structure stands here today after renovations.

Here is an interesting scene from the tower. The Officers' Club and bachelors' quarters resemble a large country club complete with the tennis courts and a golf course on the parade grounds. The Officers' Club played a key role in social events at the fort as it was host to balls and receptions. Beside the main building is a similar building that may have been officers' quarters as well. With the long sidewalk removed, only a scar remains from the water pipe that runs underground.

What a difference a century makes, well almost a century. In this c. 1910 postcard, horses can be seen outside the stables, and a neighbor had some elbow room. Today most of the wide-open spaces have been filled with single-family brick homes, which were added after the base closure. The ravine in the center was repurposed as a common area providing a walking trail, a retention pond and duck sanctuary, and a place for community get-togethers. The empty space in the foreground was once home to one of three base chapels.

View from Tower looking south, Q.M.D., Fort Sheridan, Ills.

The Water Tower and Barracks

Another view from the tower is seen in this southeastern exposure. The tents in the background of this photograph, taken in 1926, are those of the Citizens Military Training Camp (CMTC). Fort Sheridan hosted 1,600 young men for one month (August–September) and trained them as soldiers. These camps were established by Gen. Leonard Wood and were hosted nationwide in various army posts. In the foreground, the mess hall and central heating plant can be seen. The construction of the Ravines Condominiums and many new homes and townhomes altered this view dramatically.

Main Buildings of U. S. A. General Hospital No. 28, Fort Sheridan, Ill.

During World War I, Fort Sheridan constructed a hospital beginning at the barracks that spilled onto the parade grounds. It was the largest base hospital in the United States, treating both wounded soldiers and all those suffering from the great flu epidemic of 1918. It was known first as U.S.A. General Hospital No. 28 and then Lovell General Hospital. From this angle, it was easy to see the expansion in this postcard from that era. The hospital was only temporary (1918–1920), and there are no remnants of it today.

THE WATER TOWER AND BARRACKS

THE PARADE GROUNDS

On the parade grounds of Fort Sheridan, the secrets of its past are well kept under the tall oaks and manicured lawn. Over the years, it has been home to a hospital (as seen in this photograph from 1920), a chapel, a hostess house, a horse arena, and a golf course. These grounds have provided space for ice-skating, baseball games, track meets, ceremonies, speeches, and even the firing of cannons.

In this postcard dated 1918, there is a building that has proven very elusive to research. According to the title, this is the Red Cross building. At the time of World War I, a Red Cross station would be a much-needed addition for the army base.

The date of construction is not known, but this building has played an important role here. It was built on the southwest corner of the parade grounds. It is clearly seen from the air on the previous page.

Red Cross Building,
Fort Sheridan, Ill.

The post chapel is pictured here in 1930. Notice the similarity to the previous page. This a view of that same building from the east. The balcony structure and window placement gave way to the mystery. It was possibly always the chapel and just served a dual purpose during World War I. Either way, it was destroyed by fire on February 3, 1931.

This is the hostess house (1919–1943) at the northwest end of the parade grounds. Here the men could relax, read, and play checkers and chess. The hostess house provided not only hot meals but also young ladies of the YWCA for dances during the CMTC in 1926. Hostess Jessie Goodwin spent years ministering to the young men stationed at the fort. She and her volunteer Lillian Kelly made this a home away from home. They can be seen in front of the building here in this photograph from around 1920. Today the hostess house is only a beloved memory.

This 1930 photograph has a notation of "artillery firing salute" and is the epitome of the type of activities that took place here when the fort was actively utilized by the U.S. Army. The parade grounds were designed in the center and were definitely center stage in that era. While ceremonies are no longer frequently hosted here, in July 2007, an Army Reserve Change of Command Ceremony took place, and once again, the grounds were adorned with flags and flooded with folks who gathered to watch.

Without this photograph from 1945, it would be very hard to believe that the parade grounds were home to a baseball diamond. In fact, baseball leagues at Fort Sheridan date back as far as 1910. The crowds that used to assemble to cheer on their teams would have surely taken their toll on the lawn, but the quiet scene of the present day hides the evidence of any such activity under the thick green grass. (Contemporary image, courtesy of Bob Drinkall.)

CHAPTER 3

THE STARS AND STRIPES

In this 1963 photograph, the fort's flag is being raised in a ceremony. This one image seems to exemplify 120 years of military presence and patriotism. That sentiment can still be felt here today as American flags can be found flying throughout the fort. The red, white, and blue make for a beautiful contrast against the strong beige bricks. Veterans Day and Memorial Day ceremonies still take place here at the flagpole each year.

Gen. Philip Henry Sheridan (1831–1888) served under Gen. Ulysses S. Grant and Gen. William Tecumseh Sherman in the U.S. Civil War and was praised for his military genius and horsemanship. He was appointed to lieutenant general in 1869 and stationed in Chicago. Sheridan is buried in Arlington National Cemetery, but here he is forever immortalized in bronze on the west end of the parade grounds. This sculpture was commissioned by the Fort Sheridan Centennial Committee, created by sculptor Lawrence Noble, and unveiled on June 14, 1990.1

MAJ. GEN. P. H. SHERIDAN

The United States Army Color Guard marches in on a road somewhere in Fort Sheridan in this postcard from 1918. This is a military tradition that is still practiced today, as seen in this photograph of the parade down Lyster Road in July 2007, before the Change of Command Ceremony by the Army Reserve, 3rd Brigade, 75th Division.

"Color Guard," Ft. Sheridan, Ill.

"'Old Glory' over Fort Sheridan" is seen here as it was in the original location just southwest of the parade grounds. This postcard is not dated, but the height of the tower indicates that it is after 1949. The flagpole with arms that reached out to grab the earth was replaced by a new sleek, self-sustaining one and moved to the west end of the parade grounds in the center. This new location places it next to the statue of Gen. Philip Henry Sheridan himself.

"Old Glory" over Fort Sheridan, Illinois

CHAPTER 4

THE ARCHITECTURE

Brig. Gen. Samuel B. Holabird, quartermaster general of the U.S. Army, awarded the Fort Sheridan commission to his son's firm, the prominent Chicago architectural firm of Holabird and Roche. It was responsible for early skyscrapers in Chicago and has Soldier Field and 12 other downtown buildings to add to its credits. The deeply recessed and arched windows are a prominent design trait of the firm and a common feature among the buildings here at the fort.

Building No. 9, 111 Logan Loop, was built in 1890 for the fort's commander and his family. Constructed in the Queen Anne style and overlooking Lake Michigan, it was a suitable rival for those homes on the North Shore at that time and still is today. The front entryway and window were modified, as seen here, in the 1970s but have since been restored to the original design.

Looking east toward Logan Loop in this very early photograph, probably from the late 1800s, it seems as though time has actually stood still for this street. The road is dirt, and the drainage system is composed of rocks from the lakefront, but all in all, it really is not so different.

Today these homes (from right to left, buildings No. 5, No. 4, and No. 3 pictured here) are nearly the same from the front. Additions have found their way onto most, but for 120 years old, this is a well-preserved neighborhood.

The appearance of the Officers' Club (building No. 31) was a bit different in the beginning. It was one of the original buildings designed by Holabird and Roche and was constructed in 1893. After a fire in 1954, the west end was rebuilt with a relief of Gen. Philip Henry Sheridan above the doorway. Originally the Bachelor Officers' Quarters, it was also used as the open mess hall. Today it is closed and undergoing more renovations to possibly accommodate loft apartments.

Building No. 92, 3711 Leonard Wood Avenue, was built in 1905. It was originally built as lieutenants' quarters and housed a notable resident. George S. Patton Jr. was assigned to Fort Sheridan from 1909 to 1911 and lived here with his wife, whom he met in Lake Forest. The duplex structure is shown here in these two photographs, from around 1960 and again in 2006. Today it is home to two private residences.

The guardhouse or stockade (building No. 33) at 878 Lyster Road was among the first buildings to be constructed with a completion date of 1890. In 1906, the structure expanded with an addition to accommodate more prisoners. Maximum prisoner capacity was 120. In 1970, it entered into phase two of its story when it became the post's museum. It operated as such until 1993.

With the rebirth of the fort, this building went from a quiet museum to a building filled with the sound of music. It is now home to Midwest Young Artists, a school for talented young musicians. The interior photograph of one of the cells makes a dramatic contrast to the rehearsal hall that now occupies this space. Pictured here are music coach Sarah Barnes and students Zachary Robertson, Alex Miller, and Nick Kabat.

The old post bakery (building No. 34) is located on Lyster Road, which was named after Maj. William J. Lyster, the first commanding officer of Fort Sheridan (1887–1890). Apparently it was an important contributor since it was one of the first structures built here in 1890. It has had a second usage as well. It was converted into a child-care facility before the base closure. Today it is a private residence.

Next door to the bakery at 3588 Lyster Road is this little house (building No. 59). It was constructed in 1892 as an ordnance storehouse. The early photograph is from the 1960s, showing it as a military housing duplex. Today it is a single-family home. Looking closely, an addition that was added to the back of the building can be seen.

Another gem on Lyster Road is this duplex (building No. 45), constructed in 1910 as housing for noncommissioned officers. Noncommissioned officers are those highest-ranking enlisted personnel. With some modifications to the large front porch and the removal of one chimney, this now serves as a single-family home with room to spare.

Building No. 91, 3612 Lyster Road, was also built as noncommissioned officers' quarters in 1893. Neighboring the fort's guardhouse to the south, this structure was also once a duplex but has undergone renovations to accommodate a single family. From the outside it looks almost the same, except for the detached garage with a welcoming sundeck on top in the rear of the house.

The quartermaster and commissary storehouse on Lyster Road (building No. 35) was built in 1890. The arched windows are a giveaway that this was part of the original 64 buildings designed by Holabird and Roche. Over the years, it was also used as the Noncommissioned Officers' Club in the 1950s and administrative offices in the 1960s. Now it serves as private town houses.

Next to the old commissary on Lyster Road sits building No. 36. In this antiquated photograph it is listed simply as "shops." Built in 1890, it was part of the row of structures that defined Lyster Road. In later days, it was known to be a workshop of sorts. This modern-day photograph from the opposite side, or the northeast view, shows how nicely it has made the transition into private residences.

Near the south end of Lyster Road at the corner of Westover Road is building No. 38. Built in 1890 as the veterinary hospital, it once played a vital role providing care to the horses of the cavalry. The original construction included a hayloft and a loft oat bin, as seen in this interior photograph. The large entrance created easy access for the horses and wagons while the opening above the doorway was a portal for the oats.

By 1969, building No. 38 had also been used as the post's exchange, but it was finally known as the United States Post Office, Fort Sheridan. It served as the post office until 1993, when the base was closed. Unfortunately, today it is one of the few buildings left uninhabited. It was purchased but never renovated. The Fort Sheridan Homeowner's Association is currently devising a plan for this structure.

Directly across from the veterinary hospital was the home of the quartermaster stable guard. Building No. 37 is smaller than most here and quite simplistic—but that makes it no less historic. It was built in 1892 and can be seen again in the photograph on page 33. When comparing the two photographs seen here, it is obvious that it did not undergo major renovations and is beautifully preserved today.

The quartermaster stables complete the triangle at Lyster and Westover Roads. Officially known as building No. 80, it was built in 1892. The Quartermaster Department was established on March 28, 1812, for procurement of all military supplies. It stands to reason that the placement of its stables was near the row of shops. Today the old stables are home to people instead of horses. It has been renovated on the inside to accommodate two families and beautifully maintained on the outside to preserve the integrity of the fort.

Located just behind the commissary store is building No. 85. This was built in 1905 with the utilitarian purpose of the quartermaster warehouse and was later used as the commissary storehouse. This structure is surely one of the most inviting residences found here. With a porch that stretches the length of the building and American flags flying high, it is like a slice of "American pie."

Nestled into the corner at the intersection of Ronan and Lyster Roads is this duplex, building No. 46. It was built in 1890 as noncommissioned officers' housing. As seen here today, the former duplex has a single family residing in it with a large deck and garage added to the back. The placement could not be better, with a common area for a backyard and a clear view of the tower in the east. (Contemporary image, courtesy of Bob Drinkall.)

The base theater at 912 Lyster Road (building No. 180) was built in 1932. It was used as both a live theater and a movie theater. It is now home to the Fine Art Studio of Rotblatt-Amrany, owned by renowned husband and wife sculptors Julie Rotblatt and Omri Amrany. They renovated the space into a large studio, classrooms, offices, and a gallery. The front lawn is adorned by Rotblatt's creations, called *Petroushka's Journey I* and *Petroushka's Journey II*.

NON-COMMISSIONED OFFICERS' ROW
Fort Sheridan, Illinois

Sandwiched between Lyster and Sheridan Roads is where one will find this group of duplexes. Westover Road has been home to noncommissioned officers and their families since the buildings were constructed in the early 1930s. What they lack in amenities they make up for in charm. Like one big family, the families residing here share a backyard that stretches down the entire length of the street. These were the last of the military residences in the northern section of the fort.

The old granary or forage storehouse (building No. 39) was built in 1891 and is pictured probably not long after that. It was formerly a stop on the rail line that ran through Fort Sheridan to deliver grain for the horses as seen here. In later years, the granary was used as a warehouse and then eventually razed in the renovation to make way for new single-family homes that now complete this neighborhood. (Contemporary image, courtesy of Bob Drinkall.)

Taking a look at building No. 43 and its counterpart, building No. 42, in this antique photograph gives a view into Fort Sheridan in the very early days. Seeing the horses pulling a water tank makes it even more impressive that these brick structures were built without the help of heavy equipment. Today it is hard to imagine that horses of the cavalry were the residents of these beautiful buildings. The American flags that adorn them seem to reflect their pride in being part of American history.

Between the stables, the 3rd Battalion, 2nd Regiment reserve officers hold a drill in this 1917 photograph. The large stables building in the front left of the photograph is no longer here. The modern-day picture was taken about one block east of the original due to houses that now sit in that location. In the front left is building No. 62, and in the front right is building No. 63. This cross street was formerly named Robinson Road.

One of the six cavalry stables that was among the original construction in 1890 is building No. 43. This southeastern view was taken after the stables became administrative offices in the 1960s. The sign in front notes this one as the maintenance office. In the background on the left is building No. 44—a single-family house that was likely housing for stable sergeants. All are now home to private residents.

Building No. 62, originally stables, is seen here in 1970 when it was used as a service building. This view from the northeast shows the entrance from Ronan Road. Behind it sits building No. 63, and along with No. 42 and No. 43, they made a natural enclosure or arena for the horses. The original windows were particularly small and as with all the stables were lengthened during the renovation process.

Building No. 72 can be found at 75 Ronan Road, next to the stables. It was built in 1892 as housing for the stable sergeants; it is a single-family structure. Once the old screen was removed, a large front porch was revealed. A face-lift to both the front and back transforms this simple house into a modern-day beauty.

The infantry drill hall was built in 1893. It was used as an arena for drilling both horses and men in all types of weather. The back of this postcard has a postmark of February 16, 1914, and the soldier notes "O' we're having very cold weather here." In the 1940s, the hall was fitted with hardwood floors and used for recreational purposes. Today the 24,732 square feet have been reconfigured into apartments.

Drill Hall, Ft. Sheridan, Ill.

The rear or southern side of the drill hall has undergone quite a few changes as well. Open-roofed balconies have been added between the brick beams that run the length of the building. Residents can sit here and enjoy duck watching in the pond or wave to their neighbors as they make their way down the walking trail in this common area. (Contemporary image, courtesy of Bob Drinkall.)

Fire Dept. U. S. A. General Hospital No. 28, Fort Sheridan, Ill.

Built in 1893, the firehouse (building No. 79) on Whistler Road is seen here in its original state around 1915. Only a small main building existed at this point. Subsequent work was done in 1927 and may have been in reference to the wooden additions seen here from the east. Three major fires that have occurred at Fort Sheridan are the chapel fire in 1931, a laundry fire in 1932, and the Officers' Club fire in 1954.

THE ARCHITECTURE

This photograph was taken on Armed Forces Day, May 18, 1968. This is a day when all armed services are honored as one. Celebrations may include a parade or open house as shown here. Fort Sheridan has also demonstrated with helicopters and skydivers. In this current photograph of the firehouse, the last phase of construction is complete. While it still displays the name, Fire Station No. 1, it is now a private home with a warm history.

The mess hall on Whistler Road (building No. 47) played a vital role to the fort at its conception: it was the dining hall as well as the central heating plant. The smokestack rises up from the south end of the structure in this early photograph (dated sometime between 1891 and 1927). This angle is not possible today due to the addition of the townhomes just to the left. Since the base closed, this building has been vacant, but with green fencing around it, changes must be imminent. (Contemporary image, courtesy of Bob Drinkall.)

From the back, the mess hall has changed dramatically. The south wing and the smokestack have been completely removed to make way for a street that dead-ends at the firehouse in the east and winds around to the new condominiums from the west. In this photograph, it was used as an office building like most of the other structures at that time. It also served as the post's exchange.

The company kitchens, consisting of three buildings just behind the barracks, were added in 1908. They are numbered from the east, 108, 107, and this one, 106. By the time of this photograph, they have been remodeled for use as offices after the headquarters of the Fifth U.S. Army moved from south Chicago to Fort Sheridan in May 1967. The last renovation converted them into the luxury townhomes that they are today.

THE ARCHITECTURE

Looking east down Whistler Road toward the guardhouse, on the right, buildings No. 105, No. 104, and No. 103 can be seen. These buildings complete the symmetry of the southern view of the tower. They were constructed between 1908 and 1920. One of the post's chapels could be found at the end of Whistler next to the drill hall. No chapels remain at the fort today.

At the eastern end of Leonard Wood Avenue is building No. 84. It was built in 1905 for use as artillery barracks. In this photograph from the 1960s or 1970s, the sign above the double doors reads "U.S. Army, Midwest Region Recruiting Command," which shows how it rolled with the changes in this diversified army culture. Now it sits seemingly content as apartment homes providing a wonderful view of the parade grounds to its residents.

Flanking the tower on the west end of Leonard Wood Avenue is building No. 81. It was also built in 1905 as barracks and designated for administrative use in 1967. With the exception of interior work, this too looks nearly the same on the outside. A fresh coat of paint on the railings and some patio furniture on the decks and it is returned to its original purpose of housing, but now with civilian residents.

The gun shed on Ronan Road (building No. 89) is one of the more unique structures at the fort. Built in 1892 to house artillery, it has arched doorways directly across from each other on both sides of the building. Today it is refurbished into a gorgeous private home. Inside, the doorways welcome the morning sunlight from the east. On the western side, an arbor offers shade to the entrance, and company is greeted by a secret garden.

The pumping station (building No. 29) was built in 1890 in a similar style, with arched doorways along the eastern wall. Located right on the beach, its job was to pump water from Lake Michigan into the tower's water tank. In the distance, the old swimming pier can be seen just to the south. This building is currently undergoing renovations by two families who will share the spacious structure with the awesome view.

Fort Sheridan Hospital (building No. 1) was built in 1893 on Bradley Loop. In this vintage photograph, it was a welcoming place with a large veranda. Surely the view and the fresh air would be good for any ailment. The hospital also included a prisoner's cell block in the basement. There was subsequent construction on the single building in 1909 and again in 1952, as seen in this photograph after it became the post's library in 1967. The hospital was razed in the fort's renovations after 1993.

Building No. 87, or the "Dead House" as it was known, was adjacent to the hospital on Bradley Loop. This was the morgue. The cement crosses distinguish this little building from similar ones at the fort and are a symbol of respect for the dead. It was demolished in the fort's renovation, but the crosses have since been recovered. Today there is no sign of the hospital or the morgue here on Bradley Loop, only new homes that took their place. (Contemporary image, courtesy of Bob Drinkall.)

The Service Club of Fort Sheridan replaced the hostess house as a place to gather. It was built on the west side of Lyster Road in the 1940s. In this ceremony, October 29, 1984, Fort Sheridan was designated a national historic landmark. The service club can be seen across the street. This same view is considerably different today with the removal of the obsolete building after the fort's closure and the addition of new homes.

IN AND AROUND THE FORT

This chapter is all about the gates, roads, and bridges in and around Fort Sheridan. They too have a story to tell. Just like buildings, the scenery has also gone through some modifications as times have changed. A perfect example of that is captured in this photograph of the main gate around 1940.

Fort Sheridan's main gate is formally named George Bell Gate in honor of Maj. Gen. George Bell. He was a former corps area commander. The brick pillars and black iron gates served as the entry point from Sheridan Road. The George Bell Gate structure, pictured here in 2006, now greets visitors as they pass by on their way to the beach. Minus the lanterns, it has been preserved for the public to enjoy and is accompanied by informational kiosks and a map of the fort. (Contemporary image, courtesy of Bob Drinkall.)

Entrance, Fort Sheridan, Illinois

08-H2525

The entrance to Fort Sheridan was formerly located just south of where the new entrance is today. It could be found across from the McDonald's on Sheridan Road and ended at the flagpole once inside the gates. The placement of the new entrance makes a smooth transition into the fort from Old Elm Road. In this photograph, from around 1970, the Nike air missiles are a sign of the times and can be seen just inside the gates.

The south gates, or Patten Gate, on Patten Road are also significant and noteworthy. Erected in 1932, the brick pillars display plaques that tell the story. On the left, it reads, "Fort Sheridan U.S. Military Reservation." On the right, the plaque reads, "Gates presented by Mrs. James A. Patten of Evanston, Illinois as a token of good citizenship exemplified by the Civilian Military Training Camps." The plaques have been removed, but Patten Road still leads into the fort and will be the main thoroughfare for the new military housing.

Patten Road runs from the southern section of the fort, from Highwood, connecting it to the north by a bridge over the ravine. This bridge, constructed in 1883, can be seen here around 1900 with a woman posing as she was possibly taking a stroll (or a hike) down the steep incline to the pier. The bridge in its original state was quite beautiful with architectural details. It has since been replaced with a simple, utilitarian concrete structure.

On May 9, 1917, the southern end of Fort Sheridan was a construction site of new wooden barracks to accommodate the soldiers who would undergo training here. The same view is barely recognizable in the current photograph. While this book focuses on the northern area of the fort, the two are just a bridge away via Patten Road. Battery Barracks was a large brick structure that faced Patten Road just beyond the bridge, but in 2007, it was also demolished. (Contemporary image, courtesy of Bob Drinkall.)

Fort Sheridan, May 9, 1917.

On Ronan Road, a smaller ravine runs between the stables and the tower and is crossed by this bridge. It was originally made of wood, as seen on page 12. Here the E Battalion, 3rd Field Artillery soldiers cross in formation on their way to the parade grounds in 1930. This is the same street today but from farther north looking through the tower's base.

188 Placing Horizontal Frame on Double Lock Spar Bridge Fort Sheridan.

Fort Sheridan was strategically constructed between the two large ravines by the design plan of landscape architect Ossian C. Simonds (1855–1931). In this 1917 photograph, the men used only timber and rope to build this double-lock and spar bridge that leads from the parade grounds to the open field just north. Since the restoration of the ravine and forest preserve, a new bridge has been constructed using wood and modern materials to allow access to the preserves by foot and bicycle.

It is hard to believe that this is the intersection of Old Elm Road and Sheridan Road from a 1965 traffic survey. It somehow seems much earlier given the growth that has occurred in just 42 years. This photographic comparison shows how the area went from a quiet road to a major thoroughfare that begins at the entrance of Fort Sheridan and connects to Highway 41. Residents now have the Metra station and modern conveniences right at their doorstep. (Contemporary image, courtesy of Bob Drinkall.)

Fort Sheridan's railroad station seems to resemble the water tower in this photograph from 1900. It is a bit reminiscent of other stations like Lake Bluff or Kenilworth that are as charming as they are functional. But with time comes change, and upon rebuilding or renovating, simplicity seems to prevail. The old steam engine has also been replaced by the Metra train, which looks more like a silver bullet than toy locomotive.

CHAPTER 6

RECREATION
RESTORED

This antique photograph (possibly from the late 1800s) reflects a time of leisure at Fort Sheridan. Today that same feeling is echoed. Through the tremendous work of the Lake County Forest Preserves, Fort Sheridan has been restored to the tranquil days of yesteryear. This chapter focuses on the forest preserves and the beach and getting back to recreation.

A tour of Fort Sheridan today is sure to bring a smile of surprise and delight to faces of all ages. As part of the restoration, the Lake County Forest Preserves has included this outdoor exhibit that mimics a red-tailed hawk's nest. Yes, it is an enormous bird nest. Where there used to be soldiers, cannons, and horses tromping about, now there is a bird-watching sanctuary. It can be found just a short walk across the bridge leading into the preserves.

A look inside the red-tailed hawk's nest reveals the interesting activities that await the curious. With the binoculars inside the hawk's head, birds and squirrels are easy to spot from the top of the ravine. Here Jack Tucker learns about the wingspan of some different species of birds on this size comparison graph. Meanwhile his sister, Payton, perches herself atop a giant speckled egg. Located along the bike path, this exhibit is an unexpected treat for residents and visitors alike.

In this 1930 photograph, the rifle range was a busy place where the army's sharpshooters practiced their craft. Lake Michigan is the backdrop, and a large mound serves as the buffer behind the targets. The mound is still there and is seen from the road leading to the lake. This field will see one more transformation before being returned to the deer, squirrels, and other wildlife that can now safely call it home.

The firing range was replaced with a 3,500-foot airstrip during World War II. Its official name, given in the 1960s, was the Haley Army Airfield after Capt. Patrick Lawrence Haley, a helicopter pilot killed in Vietnam. The airplane hangar still sits in the field today as a reminder of its role in the past. A wood-chip walking trail through the preserves offers a glance at the silver shell in the distance through the indigenous plant life that has reclaimed the field.

The trail to the beach is like a mini field trip leading visitors on a journey of exhibits provided by the Lake County Forest Preserves, first past the main gate, then to this antiaircraft gun that sits inside the sandbag trench created to simulate the one in this photograph, from about 1940.

It seems almost unthinkable now that this dormant machine was fired over the lake during training exercises. These exhibits keep the history of the fort alive while the preservation of nature and people-friendly environment contradict its very existence.

RECREATION RESTORED

Just below the trench is another unique opportunity to explore. These viewfinders have also been installed for bird spotting, but for most untrained eyes, a small sailboat on the lake or whatever catches the attention of the viewer will do. Situated on the hillside, this makes for an ideal scenic location. Looking north it is easy to see Great Lakes Naval Training Station on the Lake Michigan shoreline. It is the nation's only U.S. Navy boot camp.

ANTI-AIRCRAFT GUN
Fort Sheridan, Illinois

The Fort Sheridan recreational beach, formerly at the end of Ravine Drive, was for military and their families only. It included a fishing pier and swimming tower. Those structures are no longer standing, and that recreational area has since been closed. At the new location, below the forest preserves, the beach welcomes visitors with open arms. This new location on Lake Michigan provides a great opportunity to soak up the sun or treasure hunt for the smooth pebbles and beach glass that are found here.

During the days of this 1940 photograph of the 61st Anti-aircraft Battery "in action" firing over the lake, this part of the shoreline was not exactly the friendliest spot on the beach. But now, Fort Sheridan's beach is ready to provide a tranquil experience to those who visit and plan to stay on land. The warnings are posted "no swimming allowed," and it is not because of the chilly lake water but rather the unexploded ordnances that may be found hiding underneath.

The last chapter would not be complete without mention of the Fort Sheridan Cemetery adjacent to the forest preserves. The first burial took place here in 1890, and the cemetery has remained active since that time. At its entry is a beautiful memorial and the burial place of Maj. Edward J. Vattman (1841–1919). He was a Catholic priest and the post's chaplain from 1887 to 1919. The cemetery has undergone some changes over the years, like the addition of the United States flag and the brick memorial, but less obvious is the number of graves in this photographic comparison between 1965 and 2007.

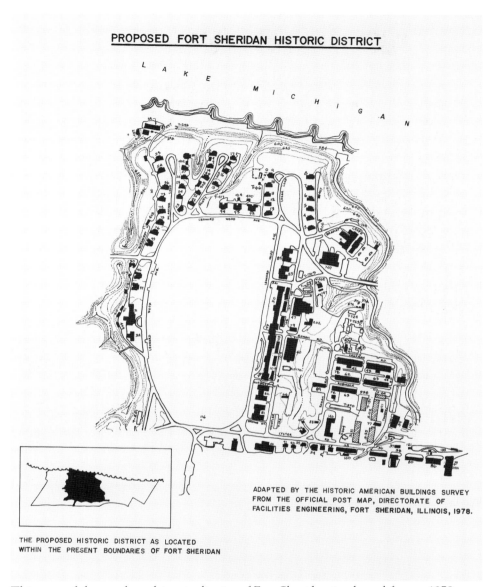

PROPOSED FORT SHERIDAN HISTORIC DISTRICT

ADAPTED BY THE HISTORIC AMERICAN BUILDINGS SURVEY
FROM THE OFFICIAL POST MAP, DIRECTORATE OF
FACILITIES ENGINEERING, FORT SHERIDAN, ILLINOIS, 1978.

THE PROPOSED HISTORIC DISTRICT AS LOCATED
WITHIN THE PRESENT BOUNDARIES OF FORT SHERIDAN

This map of the northern historic district of Fort Sheridan is adapted from a 1978 map. The historic buildings are denoted in black and numbered for reference. This has proven a useful tool in locating buildings that existed before the base closure and renovation. This map is part of the Historic American Buildings Survey Collection found online at the Library of Congress.

ACROSS AMERICA, PEOPLE ARE DISCOVERING SOMETHING WONDERFUL. *THEIR HERITAGE.*

Arcadia Publishing is the leading local history publisher in the United States. With more than 3,000 titles in print and hundreds of new titles released every year, Arcadia has extensive specialized experience chronicling the history of communities and celebrating America's hidden stories, bringing to life the people, places, and events from the past. To discover the history of other communities across the nation, please visit:

www.arcadiapublishing.com

Customized search tools allow you to find regional history books about the town where you grew up, the cities where your friends and family live, the town where your parents met, or even that retirement spot you've been dreaming about.